A LIFE OF FAITH

Stephen Waters

First published in the United Kingdom in 2025 by The Cloister House Press

ISBN 978-1-913460-96-9

Acknowledgements

I wish to thank the family members and the friends who have contributed to this tribute book without whom such a full record of Gill's achievements would not have been possible.

Also, many thanks to my sister, Jean, for typing and designing the book.

A LIFE OF FAITH

Reverend Gillian
Margaret Dallow *BA MEd*

This collection is not a full biography, more of an appreciation and an honouring of Gill's powerful influence, a written memorial to her life and achievements. Gill would have made a very fine Bishop and at the same time, deserves some recognised honour for her outstanding service to the Church and community.

Stephen Waters
5ᵗʰ December 2024

A Life of Faith

Reverend Gillian
Margaret Dallow *BA MEd*

It is 13th January 1945 and snowing. It is Mr James' birthday today but he is scarcely aware of it. His second child was due but is taking its time. Soon however, the wonder of a father holding his new-born second daughter whose birthday has turned out to be the same day as his own completely cancels any worry or concern. The snow has made the townscape glamorous hiding any signs of a war in its fifth year.

Bill James R.A.F.

Margaret Handy

1

Mr James' first born daughter was entering her fifth year, born just before Christmas – hence the name Carol. For the new bonnie arrival, it was agreed to include her mother's name of Margaret – Gillian Margaret. (Gillian sounds a little like the feminine version of William, the proud father's name.)

Gill's father was known as a very respected strong and kind man and there was always a profound understanding between father and second daughter.

So Carol and Gillian were nearly five years apart, one born at the beginning of the Second Great War and the other near its end.

Fourteen months later came daughter number three with some debate between the name of Susan and Suzanne, with a settlement on Susan. Then there was a gap of seven years before the long awaited son and younger brother, William arrived.

Early Days in Strathnairn Street

Streets in Cardiff may be named after
cities in England such as Colchester or
Ipswich but a large swathe of the city
echoes the largesse of the Earl of Bute.
The Earl's former house is across the road
from his church and is now a well known
funeral parlour. The church incidentally is
built of seven different kinds of stone. The
Earl of Bute's huge influence accounts for
the Scottish names of streets. Hence the
street of the origin of the dynamo of this
story has the name Strathnairn Street,
number 86. The family's primary school
was just across the road – St Martin's but
the future high school was a two mile walk
away in Cathays. Of course, the map of
Cardiff is littered with Welsh names,
Cyncoed etc.

Imagine older sisters, Gill was the
second in age, wheeling their little brother,
William, through all the extensive parkland
of the city starting at Waterloo Gardens –
among streets named after famous Boer
War battles – all the way to the Wild Wood

3

at the north end of Roath Lake. Children are often known for their fun but this family had an overdose of personality (and I might add, of brain power), so keep using your imagination.

I'm sure they had enough resources for sweets and ice-cream. I believe they learnt how to manage pocket money at an early age. (Their generous father called it petty cash.)

Their gifted father was a moderator in the Welsh Presbyterian Church and the family was well drilled in the faith walking to church two or three times on Sundays to Metal Street Presbyterian (in an area where streets are still named after metals – Copper, Zinc, Iron Street and so on.)

This old black and white photograph of a four or five year old girl, very pretty and engaging, writing on a toy blackboard was taken by Gill's father and even at this young

age, gives a bold impression of someone full of indomitable deter-mination. Gill had to be ambitious in life to feel truly fulfilled.

This grounding in the faith must have been very firm as shown when some seventy years later, in a very different environment of course, Gill was asked by her NHS carers to fill in a form: *Question:* What is most important to you? *Gill's answer:* To live a life worthy of Christ and to share faith in a practical way.

Throughout her life Gill was brilliant at finding exactly the right words.

**Memories of Gill
by her sister, Carol Jones**

When Gill was born, I remember at the age of five people talking about the veil over her face and I remember my mother and others saying she was sent by God.

The babies born with the amniotic sac intact are one in eighty thousand. Clearly there is a good reason physically for this 'en caul' on babies but it is not surprising that various cultures have interpreted it in different, sometimes spiritual ways. Known as born with the veil, in Gill's case it is not difficult to connect this occurrence with Gill's future career especially as one of the first women to be ordained priest in the Anglican church and in view of all her wonderful service to church and community.

Gill came to Cathays High School when I was a prefect in the fifth year. She was an industrious student and did well in all her work. Following me to Bangor she studied Theology and Welsh and followed me to teach at home. Three teachers in the family!

Gill became godmother to my first born daughter Ceri and participated in my two daughters' weddings. My daughter Ceri was at Gill's wedding with Roger Dallow in 1968.

We all had happy times together and Gill and her friend Gwenda visited Glyn and me in London several times when Glyn and I were teaching there. Later, Gill was ordained priest in St Paul's Cathedral and my family and I were so proud to be able to attend the ceremony.

When I visited my sister the day before she died she was anxious and upset.
"Have I done anything wrong?" she asked.
"Far from it," I assured her. "You are about to be taken into the arms of the Lord you have believed in all your life."
I took her by the hand and prayed and felt her relax.
"Will you be with me when it happens?" said Gill gratefully.
"Of course."

It is ever my deep regret that, through no fault of my own, I wasn't there in time, except in spirit and Gill died very peacefully after an all-night coma.

I and my family miss her so much as do so many people she came in contact with throughout her life.

Gill's father, Carol and baby Gill

Memories of Early Years
by Gill's Sister, Susan Moss

Gill and Sue

Gill was born to Bill and Peg on 13ᵗʰ January 1945. This was a very special day as it was her father's birthday. Her mum told the story that she was delivered by a devout Roman Catholic midwife who wanted Gill to be called Mary and suggested that she should be called Mary. Little did the midwife know that Gill's father was an elder in the Presbyterian Church so she was called Gill – not Gillian as she never really liked that full version. So Gillian Margaret James was her full name. Margaret after her mother.

Gill was the second daughter, closely followed fourteen months later by her sister Susan (Sue). There was a gap of seven years before the long awaited son and young brother, Will, arrived.

9

At a young age Gill's love of shopping was seen. She would spend most Saturdays with her sister Sue shopping until they dropped, often seven hours at a stretch. The favourite shop was the C&A fashion shop in Cardiff's Queen Street. There was never time, nor money for coffee in those early years.

Gill loved the ballet. Every week she would attend lessons with her school friend. She very proudly took part in a stage production at the New Theatre. Gill was dressed to resemble a tree, a green dress made by her mum.

We would enjoy our Sunday visits to our Aunty Phil who lived next door. Every Sunday morning after visiting our church we would jump over the garden wall and join our aunt and nan who lived there. We always had a welcome and some very tasty biscuits. We always had the radio on and enjoyed listening to Forces Requests. In our aunt's house we would dance and jig around to the music. This used to annoy our nan who would rebuke us and condemn us for dancing after we had just been to the 'mission'. We spent so many happy Sundays dancing and annoying our grandmother!

Gill loved school, and thoroughly enjoyed learning in the Albany Road Junior School (modern name Primary School), just opposite our house. She regularly looked forward to the weekly comic 'School Friend'. Gill loved the tales of school.

Gill's love of fashion developed in her early teens and always had a keen eye for a bargain. Sometimes this would mean touring round the shops only to go back to the original one to purchase the outfit. Several times her younger sister would borrow her outfits, without permission, only to return them to her wardrobe without Gill's knowledge!

Gill, with her younger sister, would often attend Heath Evangelical Church, especially on a Sunday evening.

Gill went to Cathays High School and after achieving 'A' level passes moved on to Bangor University. She was later to meet Roger, a young man training to be a Probation Officer. He was a keen Christian and enjoyed being with people. Together, Gill and Roger grew into strong Christians. This Christian faith kept Gill through difficult years ahead. At this time Gill, Roger and her younger sister were baptised at Pudson Baptist in Hereford.

Shortly after, Roger was diagnosed with cancer. After a valiant fight he died six months after their marriage. Gill was a very young widow but became determined to spend her life glorifying God. It was from this moment on that her life was full of activity and energy using the years to work sharing her Christian faith.

Comments from William James, Gill's brother

Gill's brother, William, underlined how devoted Gill was to her family, looking after her mother and taking her to visit the rest of the family. Everyone enjoyed memorable visits to Gill's parish in Leicestershire. We all know just how much Gill enjoyed celebrations, say at New Year, and how much she was always the joyful life and soul of the party. Gill would often give lifts to her family when they needed to catch a plane for family holidays.

William was also very keen to mention how Gill obliged him into good revision for O and A levels, the gateway to his future considerable academic achievements.

Memories from Lorraine, Gill's friend and sister-in-law

Gill was really kind. When I moved to Bristol for my first job at the Children's Hospital I stayed with Gill for a few months in her house in Wolsey Road. She would always wait up for me to return from a shift and we would sit and chat into the early hours. I quickly changed from having tea with sugar as her sugar tin had previously had salt in it! Tea would always be Earl Grey never your standard PG Tips.

Gill would often surprise me with tickets for the Ballet at the Bristol Hippodrome which I enjoyed immensely.

Gill would always get excited if we were planning a holiday and would always have a guidebook for us to borrow, and frequently provided a taxi service to and from the airport.

Gill adored the twins, William and Sarah and we enjoyed so many family holidays together with Peg and the dog Benny and later Skip.

Happy times in Penally, Manorbier, Devon and lovely visits to Buckfast Abbey; we would always come away with a fridge magnet.

So many lovely visits as a family to London and later the Vicarage at Barlestone where most years we would spend New Year's Eves together, drink lots of red wine and then end the break with a full on cooked breakfast the next morning.

We loved the trips to Barlestone and the church Harvest Festivals with Jim on the out of tune organ. The twins often took part with a reading or a prayer … special times.

Gill was so generous to let us go to the caravan whenever we wanted and would always leave us lovely wine and crisps and Easter eggs if it was Eastertime.

I loved some of her hand me downs; I still love the suede black coat she gave me

as she didn't want it any more and loved
her Clinique freebies which she would
always pass in my direction.

Gill was like a best friend to me when
my Mum died and was always supportive.

In later years we always spent
Christmas together and enjoyed it with
Stephen as well after their wedding. She
always bought over the M&S Christmas
pudding and again plenty of red wine and a
Christmas selection box for all!

Memories from Sarah, Gill's niece, daughter of William and Lorraine and twin sister to William *(Jnr)*

Firstly, I have very fond memories of Christmas and New Year spent with Aunty Gill and Nanny, and later Aunty Gill and Stephen. Every Christmas, we'd settle down for the annual (for me at least) Christmas special of Eastenders and at lunch I would write everyone name tags. Aunty Gill's would inevitably always be a joke about being the Vicar of Dibley. At New Year, William and I would have hours of fun playing in the woods before coming into a warm (her house was always warm) and raucous living room where the sound of laughter and music could be heard all the way to the parish church. As a child, her home in Barlestone felt tinged with magic: the woods, the big garden and most importantly the huge number of books! I could spend all afternoon just looking at her different books.

As a child and a teenager, I have so many fond memories of family holidays near the sea in Wales and day trips to places like Caldey Island. I will always associate Caldey Island with Aunty Gill. She would always take myself and William on countless trips to Bristol Zoo and on family days out to Buckfast Abbey. As a family, we were so fortunate to be able to use her caravan. Memories of those weekends are incredibly precious and played a huge part in helping me to retain my sanity during my Finals!

Aunty Gill was a fashion icon. I used to love seeing her new (usually purple) outfits and beautiful beads she would pair with it. She loved Peruna but was also able to rock a Sainsbury's outfit. As we were the same height and shoe size, I loved wearing some of her hand-me-downs and still have a gorgeous skirt that she insisted I have. When I was a teenager, Aunty Gill would take me shopping or to the ballet in Cardiff. Those days out were full of conversation, laughter and some dubious driving!

From conversations about fashion and hair, to conversation about theology, Aunty Gill loved to chat. Her passion for theology had a profound impact on me growing up. Watching her lead her churches, significantly influenced by decision to study theology at university. When she found out that I had received a place to read theology at Oxford, she was overjoyed. Her enthusiasm and encouragement, and determination that I would get a bike (because 'that's what you do at Oxford') will always remain with me. I treasure the study Bible and various other books that she and Stephen bought me.

As an adult, engaged and then married to Dave, it was wonderful to spend time with both Aunty Gill and Stephen. We enjoyed staying with them in Cardiff and going for meals out. We both felt there was much to learn from their wisdom; conversations with them would always cover a wide range of topics. We were so pleased that Aunty Gill was well enough to read and serve communion at our wedding. A special part of our day.

It is not an exaggeration to say that my love to travel, appreciation of the finer things in life (David Lloyd!}, love for

Nutcrackers(!), collection of books about the Bible, fascination with Theology and my own faith were influenced greatly by Aunty Gill.

*Gill with twin nephew, William
and niece, Sarah*

Gwenda Francis – Memories of Gill at Cathays High School

In September 1956 I was sitting on the floor of the assembly hall at Cathays High School for Girls, along with around ninety other new girls waiting to find out in which form they would spend the next few years. Next to me was a girl I had never met before and she had a wonderful ponytail. I was envious of the ponytail as my mother was a great believer in short hair. The girl of course was Gill and we found that we were going to be in the same form – 1W. We were friends for the next seven years.

Gill and I had several things in common. We liked school, we liked our school uniform and we both wanted to do our best at everything. Getting top marks in tests was very important to Gill. She was well-behaved in class (well, most of the time) and didn't really enjoy it when some of the girls 'messed around' in the French class.

There was a system in our school whereby it was possible to earn a 'posture girdle'. This was a yellow sash to wear around your school tunic to denote that you were well-groomed and had good posture. The sashes were awarded at the end of each term and the day soon came when Gill was able to proudly wear the yellow sash.

Our days at Cathays High School came to an end in the summer of 1963 but by the end of September we found ourselves on an early train to Bangor where we were to study at the University College of North Wales. We stayed friends during the years I was in Bangor, although we were studying totally different subjects.

After that we went our separate ways but always kept in touch.

I was very happy when Gill came back to live in Cardiff, and we were able to resume our friendship.

Pontypridd *(Everyone calls it Ponty)*

After a degree at Bangor followed by teacher training, Gill obtained a post at a tough school in Pontypridd, Cardiff. The headmaster in his unwisdom, or as it turned out his wisdom, gave Gill the charge of Class 4C, almost certainly the most difficult class in a difficult school. The boys probably looked at school as though it were an enemy from the middle class trying to do them down.

A crowd of strapping youths eyed their not very tall but very well groomed and, yes, glamorous new teacher, pointedly. Gill had come to teach RE and Welsh. "We don't believe in God and we don't wanna learn Welsh," declared their spokesperson. They obviously were not going to pay attention or bother to help Gill.

They had made a big mistake miscalculating the great force of Gill's powerful personality.

Gill stared them down waiting for silence. Her strong gaze, they felt, was piercing their very souls. It took twenty minutes before an (unusual) respectful silence pervaded the schoolroom.

That is how 4C began to lean RE and some Welsh, but of course, they learnt much more. Because of Gill's character and her profound humanity, because of her constant unflinching determination, the class could learn about real life and confidence in themselves. Gill's deep faith was more than just belief; it breathed from her very presence, her words and her actions and from her uncanny way of seeing into the heart of things and of people.

The stay in Pontypridd High was not to be a long one but when Gill left for a Sixth Form post in Hereford, grown tough youths, probably from difficult backgrounds, shed tears.

Hereford

Life in Hereford Sixth Form College really opened up for the young teacher. Not simply as far as her career was concerned for it was here that she met her future husband who gave her the surname that she was known as for the rest of her life – Roger Dallow.

Roger and Gill attended the same Baptist church. Gill used to say in later life that she was baptised three times; once as an infant, once by immersion and once in the spirit.

"Bless me in the Spirit," requested Gill after the Toronto blessing - "don't make a space for me to fall, I'm not going to!"

However, (a very big however) back to Hereford - Gill had met Mr Right. Roger was highly gifted and Gill's perfect companion. With high academic qualifications, he was set to work in his father's insurance company. Gill and Roger were engaged to be married. Roger had proposed romantically during a trip in the Vale of Glamorgan – somewhere between Llantwit Major and Aberthaw. Llanwit Major has St Illtud's Church, built on the site of the oldest monastic college in Britain founded by St Illtud c.508AD. Aberthaw boasts the oldest pub in Wales, 'The Blue Anchor' which preserves its fine medieval atmosphere. Gill would point out to family and friends that "This is where Roger proposed to me."

The marriage was planned and preparations began. However, Roger was diagnosed with lymphoma which in the sixties had little chance of being cured although chemotherapy would delay the deep sadness of everyone.

A difference of opinion arose in some members of the two families about whether the marriage should go ahead. But we need to remember the deeply embedded determination of Gill's character and undoubtedly that also of her fiancé.

So the marriage took place with all the usual ceremony and celebration – and also the honeymoon in Lynton and Lynmouth famous for the river, the sea, the rocky headland, the vast woodlands, the valley of rocks, Lee Abbey, and picturesque houses once visited by famous romantic poets such as Coleridge who would walk together for miles on the Devon coast and in the beautiful Devon countryside.

Five and a half months after the wedding Roger died in hospital with his devoted and passionate wife by his side.

Gill's sister Sue was also nearby. Gill and Sue were very close in age and in their care for one another.

Gill never really talked about her grief except to talk of Roger from time to time. Perhaps her grief was too deep for words and there never will be enough tears.

What Gill achieved since the death of her husband seems almost like a kind of defiance, so powerful and momentous was her future to be.

Bristol and the South West

Gill's next occupation was at the prestigious girls' school known then as Colston Girls' School, now Montpelier School, where she still had time to study for an M.Ed. to add to her degree and diploma. Thus was this born teacher qualified for quite high positions in the education world and beyond.

More significant however was her membership of Redlands Church where she made strong and lasting friendships particularly with her future sister-in-law Lorraine and with her great friend Elaine.

So strong was Gill's outgoing personality that one vicar tried to rein in her activities. Really, he should have noticed her qualities of leadership. However Gill took charge of serving coffee and especially of encouraging students through that service and winning many followers for the Gospel and to membership of that very lively church. Gill had the ability to befriend everyone she met and making them feel good about themselves. In fact she was always a brilliant judge of character and gifted at understanding people. Having met Gill people always remembered her vivid presence, her commitment and love of fun.

The highly gifted preacher Rev'd Tony Baker, a later vicar of Redlands, understood Gill's special influence and the two formed a life-long friendship. Gill had more friends at home and abroad and in various congregations, communities and neighbourhoods than anyone knew.

Still based in Bristol our firebrand worked next for the Scripture Union, driving from school to school in her Ford KA setting up Christian Union clubs with material from Scripture Union, a band of brothers and sisters who taught and spread the Gospel simply and first of all by how they treated one another and

Gill, 1996

all whom they met. The joy of life itself and the inspiration of scripture flourished in their hands. Among them you knew the meaning of real fellowship. Here Gill made more lasting friendships including David and Hilary Blair and Lindsay Brown.

The area Gill covered was spread across South West England and some of South Wales. Her office was in the grounds of that beautiful building, Wells Cathedral.

Lecturer

This broad sweep through Gill's life and times has now reached the nineties where we find Gill as Director of Training at what was then known as the London Bible College, now the London School of Theology. Again the keynote was lasting friends for instance the inspired Rev'd Peter Hicks and his wife Dorothy.

Gill's work involved lecturing, of course, but also guiding students in church youth work. Gill published two books about Youth Work. Even quite recently her book '*Touching the Future*' is still

31

available on Amazon. This remains a very stimulating and unusual account of what it means to be a Youth Worker in today's churches.

Ordination

Gill had been led to request ordination once before but had decided to decline even though considered highly suitable. So when Gill felt the call would not go away she re-applied. Of course the first question then was "Why did you not go ahead the first time?" But then directors or ordinands try to put you off in order to test the genuineness of the call.

So Gill completed training from Oakhill College and in 1996 was ordained in St Paul's Cathedral with the guidance of the powerful personality of Bishop of London, Richard Chartres who taught her to learn the communion service prayers by heart so that you were facing the con- gregation while celebrating. St Paul's in architecture and music has everything to make the occasion grand and inspiring. It was also a wonderful occasion for members of Gill's family.

Gill ordained in St Paul's Cathedral by the Bishop of London, Richard Chartres, 1996

Curacy in West Ealing

After ordination (1996 and 1997) Gill
became a non-stipendiary minister at
St John and St James Church, West Ealing.
The effect Gill had during this time can
best be illustrated by a version of *'The
Sound of Music'* applied to Gill, written by
a gentleman from this church named
Godfrey Rust and entitled *'The Sound of
Dallow'*. It is very entertaining and
amusing but, at the same time, contains a
huge appreciation of what Gill could do
and of who she was – and still is in loving
memory of so many people. The copy is
signed "Love, Godfrey". And that is the
root of this short biography. Gill inspired
love in all whom she met – individuals and
groups. Her company was joyful and very
memorable. That Gill was full of
personality would still be an
understatement.

Actually Gill's favourite musical and favourite music was '*The Sound of Music*' which is fun with the very serious undertone of escape from Nazi oppression. For all her vitality the essence of Gill's psyche was that her laughter was never superficial.

Farewell from Curacy at
St John's, West Ealing
Used with the kind permission of Godfrey Rust

THE SOUND OF DALLOW

Good evening. Today we bring you a preview of a sensational new stage show based on the life of one of the century's most colourful clerics. *The Sound of Dallow* opens for what is expected to be a long run next month at the Theatre Royal, Barlestone and it is appropriate that the music for this part-fact, part-fictional account of the career of the woman they call *The Vamp from the Valleys* should be based on shows that starred one of her childhood heroines, Julie Andrews.

In rehearsals the show was at different times going to be called *My Fair Curate* and *Gilly Poppins* before the final title was chosen. Indeed, the way that Gill Dallow's career followed that of her idol is quite uncanny. Few people know that the two were actually in competition for the film part of Maria in *The Sound of Music*.

37

Dallow tragically lost out at the final hurdle because every time she ran to the top of a hill and burst into song what came out was *Guide me O Thou Great Jehovah.*

The part of Gill Dallow in the stage production is taken by Joanna Myers in her Barlestone debut and the show opens with a young, untested Gill Dallow, newly out of theological college and with eschatological imperatives still very much on her mind, wandering in the flower market and thinking of what the future may hold...

All I want is a church somewhere
Not too far from Trafalgar Square
Which needs some loving care
Oh wouldn't that be beautiful?
Lots of home groups for me to lead
Lots of lessons for me to read
Long hymns, long prayers, long creed
Oh wouldn't that be beautiful?

Oh so beautiful taking services
  week after week
I would never leave unless All Souls
  invited me down to speak ...

Just a stone's throw from LBC
Not too liberal theology
Perhaps a curacy
Oh wouldn't that be beautiful
* beautiful,*
Beautiful (there's pretty for you.)

So Dallow comes to St John's, West
Ealing, a church which after a hundred
years of male vicars and curates is
desperately in need of a woman's touch.

She quickly brings a new sense of order
into the place. Although only coming to
the parish for a day or two each week, her
occasional appearances in Ealing become
likened to the whirlwind visits of Margaret
Thatcher at her peak to ailing factories in
depressed industrial areas. Her aides and
entourage struggle to keep up with her as
she races from pastoral visits to funerals, to
tea at the vicarage, to diocesan committees,
to home groups, finishing the day with that
brief, eighty mile an hour dash back to her
Northwood home, tireless in service,
careless for her own well-being or for the
contents of the Highway Code.

How it must have reminded her of her heroine, Maria, as she stood before that congregation, reminding her of nothing more that those lovable but disobedient von Trapp children, needing to learn how a church should really be run.

Lets start at the very beginning
A very good place to start
When you read you begin with ABC
But at church you begin with you
*   and me, you and me*
The congregation happens to be
*   you and me, you and me...*

(All right, I'll make it easier ...
*   listen...)*

Me – a priest, a female priest
Ray – that covenant form's not done
Mark – you chair the PCC
Steve – your flies are undone
Don – you're preaching Sunday night
Joan – please could you make the tea?
Mike – you must turn off the light
*   and that will bring us back to me!*

Me – a priest, a female priest
Gary – please rearrange the chairs
Wei Hei – the DCC minutes are late
   again
young people – now its time to go
   downstairs
David Conacher – take the collection
   in the next hymn please
Graham Bothamley – we'll have the
   music on the OHP
Karen Taylor-Burge – please have the
   children ready after the Peace
and you can bring them back to me... !

Her impact is felt in all corners of
St John's life. A new office answering
machine is installed with tapes that will
take messages of more than ninety minutes
at a time. But nowhere do the winds of
change blow more strongly than in the
music group. This once dynamic ensemble
had fallen into a sorry state.

After years of neglect during which its
repertoire was entirely drawn from a copy
of the Spring Harvest Songbook for 1982
from which all Dave Bilbrough songs had

41

recently been mysteriously removed, the music group finds itself faced with a service leader who actually selects music, and even more remarkably tells the musicians what it will be four days in advance. For some, this new regime is almost too much to take …

I'm leading worship in the morning
Got to be there at five past nine
I'm feeling too sick
Cos Gill's choosing music
So get me to the church on time.

We're playing Kendrick in the
     morning
Don't care if some of them don't
     rhyme
The singing is crusty
The guitars are rusty
So get me to the church on time.

If I am leading then let us pray
If I'm rehearsing (well that'll be the
day...)

We're singing Youth Praise in the
     morning

(if you're under forty you can mime)
  pass me my hankie
at least it's not Sankey
and get me to the church on time.

Gill wants tradition in the morning
Gerald is coming to his prime ...
She likes the organ
  cos she's from Glamorgan
So get us to the church, Get us to the
  church
Be sure to get us to the church on time.

But Gill is not all business and bustle.
Between hairdressing appointments,
sermon preparations and appearances
before the magistrates for minor traffic
offences, we see glimpses of a sensitive
woman searching for her true identity.
This is touchingly revealed in an
impromptu visit she pays one day
downstairs to the young peoples' groups,
where she finds some children crying upset
because Mark Sheard has stolen their teddy
bears to use as visual aids in a corporate
video he is shooting. Gill draws them
round, and shares with them her secret of
happiness ...

News spots and song sheets and
orders of service
Men who aren't tall and don't make
me feel nervous
Telling the music group just what to
sing
These are a few of my favourite
things...

Tuesdays in Northwood and Sundays
in Ealing
Songs from the valleys that choirs sing
with feeling
Suits by designers and dangly earrings
These are a few of my favourite
things...
Pictures and nick-nacks and
paraphernalia
Globetrotting missions to visit
Australia
Master Sun holidays taken in Spring
These are a few of my favourite
things...

When the clock stops,
When the mouse bites
When the traffic's slow

44

I simply remember my favourite things
And then I don't feels so low ...

People who visit and like what I feed
*   them*
Radio mikes that will work when I
*   need them*
Big parking spaces when I'm motoring
These are a few of my favourite
*   things ...*

Keys that aren't lost and Emmaeus
*   group meetings*
Friends from the past sending wishes
*   and greetings*

Hosting a dinner that goes with a
*   swing*
These are a few of my favourite
*   things ...*

Giving egg-timers for timing the
*   sermin*
Houses with tenants and no mice or
*   vermin*
Hope for the future whatever it brings
These are a few of my favourite
*   things ...*

When the time flies
When the job's done
When I have to leave
I simply remember my favourite things
And then I don't have to grieve.

Of course, all successful shows have
love interest, and this is no exception,
although it is love of a secret, unrequited
kind. As Gill's meteoric star blazes across
St John's, in the pew sits a dazzled but
tongue-tied young man, tragically aware
that it is their destiny never to be lovers
because of the unbridgeable gulf that lies
between them…

I have often sat in this aisle before
But the sermon never seemed to raise
   a smile before
All at once am I seven heavens high
Knowing I'm in the church where you
   preach.

People stop and stare they don't
   bother me
Even tho' you're four foot ten and I
   am six foot three
Oh what joy if I only caught your eye

Sitting here in the church where you
preach.

And oh that towering feeling
Of looking down and hearing how
*   your words will please*
The overpowering feeling
To know your eyes might any moment
*   meet my knees ...*

Are there horse-chestnut trees in the
*   Avenue?*
For you've conkered me with charm
*   and passion, haven't you?*
O how thrilled I'd be – please look up
*   to me*
Sitting here in the church where you
preach!

Under the watchful theological gaze of
Ian Fishwick, played imaginatively here in
a change of career by Kevin Keegan, and
aided by the young ambitious curate Mark
Bratton – a part handled I thought well, if a
little overacted, by Brian Blessed – Gill's
preaching has indeed gone from strength to
strength. How had this transformation
come about? ...

Well boys, at first I was nervous and
could hardly string three points
together, but then one day I was
introduced to a word that changed my
life ...

SUPERCHARGED-EVANGELISTIC-ALPHA-
CHARISMATIC
Even though the thought of it
    may sound a bit fanatic
If you say it fast enough it makes you
    quite ecstatic
SUPERCHARGED-EVANGELISTIC-ALPHA-
CHARISMATIC

Because I was afraid to speak in
    church without a hat on
One day I took a lesson from the
    wisdom of Mark Bratton
He said it didn't matter much what
    words you really used
As long as they were long enough to
    leave the church confused...

SUPERCHARGED-EVANGELISTIC-ALPHA-
CHARISMATIC
Even though the thought of it may
    sound a bit fanatic

48

If you say it fast enough it makes you
  quite ecstatic
SUPERCHARGED-EVANGELISTIC-ALPHA-
CHARISMATIC

So now my every sermon's full of
  grace and hermeneutics
The formula's so simple I can write it
  up in two ticks

A Bible verse, two words in Greek's
  enough for making may-hem
And finish with a quote from someone
  Welsh or Billy Gra-ham ...

SUPERCHARGED-EVANGELISTIC-ALPHA-
CHARISMATIC
Even though the thought of it may
  sound a bit fanatic
If you say it fast enough it makes you
  quite ecstatic
SUPERCHARGED-EVANGELISTIC-
AL...PHA...CHAR...IS...MA...TIC

The impact of such a woman in the
church is remarkable. Inspired by her
example, dozens of women rush to take up
holy orders. And yet, in spite of it all, the
source of her charismatic appeal remains

49

an enigma, a question to which there is no
ultimate answer. In a rousing climax to
the show, some of the newly-ordained
from the congregation join in tribute to her
successes, and bewilderment at the
contradictions of her character...

She'll turn up right on time and then
     she'll find she's lost her key
She changes round the service and
     ignores the OHP
And underneath her cassock she
     wears skirts above the knee
She's surely not the clergyman we're
     used to ...

I'd like to say a word on her behalf
Then say it Joan
She makes me laugh ...

How do you solve a puzzle like Gill
     Dallow?
How do you catch a cloud and pin it
     down?
How do you find a word that isn't
     shallow?
A flibbertigibbet a will-o-the-wisp
     a clown!

*Many a thing you know you'd like to
 tell her*
Many a thing she ought to understand
*But how do you make her stay and
 listen to all you say*
*How do you keep a wave upon the
 sand?*
*How do you solve a puzzle like Gill
 Dallow?*
*How do you hold a moonbeam in
 your hand?*

When I'm with her I'm confused
Out of focus and bemused
And I never know exactly where I am!
Unpredictable as weather
She's as flighty as a feather
She's a darling!
She's a demon!
She's a lamb!

She'll outpester any pest
Drive a hornet from its nest
*She could throw a whirling dervish
 out of whirl*
She is gentle, she is wild
She's a riddle, she's a child
She's a headache, she's an angel

51

She's a girl!

How do you solve a puzzle like Gill
Dallow?
How do you catch a cloud and pin it
down?

How do you find a word that isn't
shallow?
A flibbertigibbet, a will'o'the'wisp,
a clown!

Many a thing you know you'd like to
tell her
Many a thing she ought to understand
But how do you make her stay and
listen to all you say
How do you keep a wave upon the
sand?
How do you solve a puzzle like Gill
Dallow?
How do you hold a moonbeam in your
hand?

All good things come to an end, and
Gill's tenure at St John's is done, her
clerical shirts packed away and her Harry
Secombe CDs put into storage in

preparation for her next career move. A
small, sleepy rural village called
Ambridge, sorry Barlestone, waits
unsuspecting in the Midlands for the
arrival of their new vicar. As the curtain
falls, Gill pauses while shopping for a
dozen new pairs of earrings in the
Broadway Centre and again we see as one
story ends, another begins.

All I want is a church somewhere
Somewhere rural like Leicestershare
Which needs some loving care
Oh couldn't that be Barl-e-stone?
Much too quiet to make advance?
No endeavour and no romance?
Just give me half a chance
Oh wouldn't that be Barl-e-stone?
Barl-e-stone, Barl-e-stone,
  Barl-e-stone
(Ah that's what women priests can do
  for you.)

Godfrey Rust, 5th December 1998
With humblest apologies to Rodgers,
Hammerstein, Lerner and Loewe

Godfrey Rust, 5ᵗʰ December 1998
With humblest apologies to Rodgers,
Hammerstein, Lerner and Loewe

53

St Giles Church, Barlestone, Leicester

Barlestone Parish

St John and St James Church were certainly very sorry to see Gill move on to her next experience or, to be more accurate, the experience of the people Gill would come to serve. This was the diocese of Leicester as priest-in-charge of Barlestone Parish (near the historical site of Bosworth Field).

Until this time Gill had really been a city dweller including two capitals but Barlestone was a large country village, where Gill's Vicar's Warden was a very capable lady farmer and a great asset to St Giles Church. Gill being Gill organised her church extremely well, was a very effective preacher and knew who to choose for what job. Many friendships were formed. One close friend was where Gill went to relax over a glass (or two) of red wine. Then there was Glyn and Pam Bowen, Glyn being the son of a Welsh farmer. Glyn's enthusiasms, by his own confession, were church and rugby. He also was glad, he would say, as an 'economic migrant' to meet someone who could "speak proper" – meaning someone who spoke with an incisive Welsh accent.

Gill was, of course, proud of her Welsh origins. We all needed to learn the story of fifteen-year-old Mary Jones who, in 1800, walked twenty-six miles to Bala so that she could buy a Welsh bible, for which she had saved for six years.

Of course Gill was a Bible fan having worked for Scripture Union amongst other things and a very qualified Bible commentator but her interest in rugby was nothing to do with the game. It was everything to do with the national anthem ceremony at the beginning of the game and especially with the emotion of the hwyl fawr of the Welsh spectators.

When Gill returned in later life to Barlestone it was clear that she had been almost like an institution. You didn't have to go to church necessarily to know Gill. Her Anglican calling meant she served the church and the community (for which she really deserved an MBE or OBE).

Gill of course still had her specialised knowledge of youth work in school and church and was Diocesan Advisor for Youth Work. Schools loved her visits. After all she was a born teacher and understood children's spirituality.

Fun and irony never went away with Gill. She loved to tell the story of the morning service when the aged organist was playing one hymn and the people were singing another!

At the same time there were very difficult times such as dealing with the loss of a nine year old girl in a traffic accident.

Parents who lose children are never really consoled and Gill felt their pain as much as they did.

Gill's mother was developing some old age problems and Gill was the only single member in her immediate family so felt she should return to Cardiff to care for her mother.

Her influence on church, community and on the youth work in the diocese had been overwhelming. And as far as people were concerned, Gill had a powerful gift for what others might call networking. In Gill's case it was getting to know people and remembering them, knowing what they could do best, helping them to appreciate who they were. Gill had such powerful influence for good.

*Gill went back to visit her friends in Barlestone
with Stephen in September 2014*

Return to Cardiff

Gill's life had become all change. First, leaving her parish in Leicestershire where her ministry and community service with her vivacious nature had all been so much appreciated. Secondly the house in Northwood where Gill had lived while working at the London Bible College, this fine city house, which had Gill's house designing all through, now had to be sold.

Back in Cardiff, Gill settled in the family home in Penylan in order to look after her mother Margaret, known as Peggy.

Gill with her Mum and twins, nephew William, and niece Sarah.

Of course, Gill needed a church and was passionate about belonging to St Mark's, Gabalfa, and so became for the next thirteen years Associate Minister of St Mark's and of its partner church St Philip's, Tremorfa.

St Philip's was a conventional district supported by St Mark's. The Rev'd Bob Capper, vicar of St Mark's was also responsible for St Philip's which was thought of as a community church reaching out into a disadvantaged area with its Baptist Church, its African Church, known as the Garden of the Lord, its Primary and Secondary school. Gill always had good relations with all of these and especially with the teachers and pupils of the primary Baden Powell School where she was a close personal friend of the headmistress and a valuable governor. In fact, under her vicar's guidance, Gill was as good as a parish priest to Tremorfa. Gill had already understood the role of parish priest and was already an expert in children's work with extensive experience.

This wasn't all. The Archbishop had found her a job in Cardiff Bay as Chaplain to the Welsh Assembly which Gill took very seriously. Every week she would visit the Welsh Senedd, meeting each member with understanding and support as well as attending public events.

One of these events was Mariners' Memorial Day, a grand occasion with brass band and open air service. Gill would very sociably meet the local rabbi and imam who would pray in Hebrew and Arabic. Gill's clear melodious voice would echo the Christian prayers across the bay. Gill was understanding as well as amusing (don't forget she loved fun) when the imam told her apologetically that he could not shake hands with her because she was a woman; significant really because Gill was among the first women to be ordained.

Gill was also, for a time, a very active chaplain to the Youth Sea Cadets.

During these early days back in Cardiff, as busy as they were for Gill, another development began to take place. Gill had taken her mother to a Christian Hotel in St Briavels, Wye Forest for New Year in 2009. A visitor, a retired teacher from England, was waiting in the lounge for supper to be announced and glancing out of the window he saw an eye-catching well dressed woman crossing the courtyard arm in arm with an older lady – Gill and her mother. He watched them enter the lounge and offered his seat. That man was me, and from that moment Gill and I seemed unable to stop talking, swopping life histories amongst other subjects. We arranged to meet a week later in Cardiff.

This meeting began a close association of mutual help and support. I visited Gill and her mum often in Northwood and Cardiff.

"You haven't come to see me. You've come to see Gill," remarked Gill's mum on one occasion.

We supported one another in so many ways over nearly two years with outings, gardening and in everyday events including Gill's impressive church work. St Mark's partner church, St Philip's, a small struggling church in a dis-advantaged area was in dire need of some of Gill's electricity.

There was an exciting visit to Llanberis and Mount Snowdon as well as a momentous trip to New York ending with a trip by pony and trap and the driver took a photograph of the two seated together in Central Park. In the film *Pretty Woman*, Richard Gere as Mr Lewis recited a Shakespeare sonnet to Julia Roberts as Vivian Ward. Gill was sixty-three years old at the time and I was nearly ten years older. Had we been in love when we were younger, Central Park was the obvious place to propose. Neither Gill nor I knew where our love for one another was going. The truth was I should have had more initiative. How-ever, on return to the UK, there was a realisation that we should fulfil our love in the proper way.

My rather matter of fact proposal was a little unromantic, probably through nervousness about our ages.

When Roger had proposed all those years ago, Gill must have replied with a yes straightaway. This time Gill was about to go on a pilgrimage to Jordan under the guidance of Archbishop of Wales, Barry Morgan, so I was left in a two hour interview with Gill's vicar the Rev'd Canon Bob Capper. Could there be a second Mr Right for Gill?

Gill and I spent over £100 discussing our future by international mobile phone.
On the plane home Gill was privileged to be able to ask advice of the Archbishop about whether to marry again. His advice was short.
"Go with your heart!"

So there came a yes!

Engagement photo courtesy of Woman's Weekly

Back home Bob Capper said he would take Gill's service that day while we went to buy rings in the Celtic jewellers in Pontypridd. However, no longer did this jeweller stock the Celtic and so we were advised to try Porth.

Porth turned out to be quite an event. Gill so loved to study the market before purchasing, so a number of possibilities were spread out before us on the counter. Porth was a small Welsh town where everyone knew everyone else. People seemed to have picked up on the fact that two older people were becoming engaged. Advisers came in and set about helping with the choice. One about to become a fiancée was always entertained by people. We returned to Cardiff joyful and in wonder. The wedding ring is now gratefully in the possession of Gill's eldest sister, Carol, the engagement ring is proudly owned in memory by her sister, Sue, and Lorraine, Gill's sister-in-law, such a close friend through the years, is so glad to have the eternity ring.

A Sad Event

Before Gill and I reached our engagement, a very sad event had taken place.

Some time after a ninety-first birthday party in a summer garden, Gill received a 4am telephone call from a respite centre informing her that her mother had died. Her vicar Bob Capper showed his out-standing pastoral care by phoning Gill for support very early that morning. The deep sadness was doubled because Gill's mother could not now be at her daughter's second wedding.

Marriage

Our marriage took place on 14th October 2011 at St Mark's Church, Cardiff, with Gill's very good friend Bob Capper officiating.

Gill showed what a great organiser she was with her own (second) wedding. All members from both families of course, plus Gill's many, many friends and acquaintances from activity areas of her past life, filled St Mark's Church and

St David's Hotel for an exceptionally grand occasion.

After much probing and pondering around the choice of venue for the honeymoon, we considered the Mediterranean and the Adriatic, before deciding on Dubrovnik. The time of year was well into autumn which took away some of the sunshine, but opened up beautiful seascapes and Dubrovnik is a very picturesque, medieval town, touristy but unspoiled.

Former Yugoslavia, now divided into independent states, is well known in modern times for war and slaughter. However, all is peaceful and restored. Muslim Mostar with its famous bridge was memorable and mostly looking for tourists.

The day we visited was depressing mainly because of the rain. Montenegro was much happier but still mainly a tourist centre.

There was some disappointment about the honeymoon. The advertised beach was a concrete platform with reclining chairs overlooking the sea. I remember Gill's wonderful dress sense and how much she enjoyed shopping – even in Dubrovnik Airport, an expert in reading markets anywhere and always bargaining with great skill. I felt that Gill would have made a very good business woman as well as an outstanding minister of faith.

We put right the slight disappointment about the short honeymoon soon after by flying first to Paris and then far across the Indian Ocean to Mauritius - l'île Maurice where the main language is French. Here

we felt we were having a second honeymoon with spacious, atmospheric hotel, picturesque gardens, private beach, swimming pool, outings by sailing boat on a turquoise sea with views of brightly coloured tropical fish – and dolphins sporting.

During a boat trip the wind sprang up and the sea became rough. The tourists became anxious but the sailors in charge exclaimed
"This is now really exciting, we'll use just the sails and turn off the engine."

The squall didn't last long but long enough to blow my hat away into the sea. The sailors turned the boat round and fished the hat back with a boathook. They had to look after their tourists.

Mauritius was once French but when Britain took over the island with all its sugar plantations, they still kept the French language for administration.

2012 was an Olympic year so Gill asked me to see if the hotel could tune into the commentary. This they managed and we were grateful. "Translate! Translate!" challenged Gill but who can keep up with the incredible speed that French sports commentators rattle along?

When we reached Paris on the way back, a small group of managers met us saying the baggage-handlers were on strike. They said they would help, joking as they went.
"Oh no!" argued the pilot, "I want all this baggage checked."

When a delay is ended you might forget how long it was, but when on Easyjet you might be reminded when the stewards reached the middle of the plane, where we were seated, they had run out of food and drink. Gill was exasperated but then you have to laugh. So we arrived home hungry. I remember how the airline had lost our luggage on the outward journey. Nevertheless this was a memorable and wonderful second honeymoon in spite of these very minor, even entertaining, drawbacks.

Some Activities in Tremorfa

It has to be remembered importantly that during her time, even during her second marriage, Gill had been an influential member of the House of Clergy (as secretary) and also a committee member of the Evangelical Alliance, both meeting in London. Once settled in Cardiff, Gill also became a highly valued member of Baden Powell Primary School governors. Two of her best friends were the headmistress and the Brownie leader. Gill often accompanied the Brownies on their camps and visits and they would attend church for parades, christingles and nativity plays. It was a great occasion when two classes from the school would arrive for a very joyful visit.

The vicar of St Mark's organised on a Tuesday at St Philip's what was known as Messy Church, craftwork and games – so often with disadvantaged families taking part and Gill was highly involved with this contact with the community.

Gill organised other events in
St Philip's. The church won a diocesan
prize to initiate a youth club. This club
became very successful and was very
popular with the children. Here the
tremendous support of the vicar was so
much appreciated. He was the incumbent
of St Philip's with St Mark's. He had not
really thought that Gill would do so much.
Bob Capper was responsible for St Philip's
as a conventional district with Gill's input,
the area was run and organised just as a
parish with all the usual organisation of
PCC and church wardens with proper
returns to the diocese at the end of the year.

For the youth and other events to do
with St Philip's, there was great support
from Mr Mal Short, a leader and very
accomplished musician, together with his
future wife Elizabeth, and also the Rev'd
Chris Frost with his filming and musical
prowess (not to mention his fine
preaching). There was a very popular and
enjoyable home group in Mal's nearby
house.

Weddings in St Philip's could be very intriguing. A couple arranged to marry and then asked if we could supply witnesses. This meant that a total of six people only were present.

"I wanted to surprise my mother with the certificate on Christmas Day," confessed the bride.

On another occasion an estranged husband arrived at Gill's home to ask for help.

"We are fighting all the time often over the children or about money. We need a divorce settlement of some kind."

"Well, you need a lawyer," was advised. The answer was a shock surprise.

"But I can't read or write," admitted the forlorn man.

Somehow Gill managed to reassure him that it wouldn't make any difference or disadvantage him.

Tremorfa had quite a few people whose schooling had not been a great success – poor family background, dyslexia, ADHD and truancy to name a few examples of why.

The area was known as difficult but it did have a library, a football field and a (scruffy) park. Three schools and three churches served the area in its needs.

On the far east side was a large superstore and over the road a sizeable gypsy encampment.
"We are not travellers like the ones over the way," boasted their representative. "Neither are we posh gypsies like the ones near Newport."

The gypsy wedding was a great event. The church was throbbing with colourful people and bewildered non-gypsy visitors.
When the signing of the register started, nobody stayed to witness or listen to the music but preferred to block the street outside and keep the highly decorated horses and carts company.

Tremorfa had a general friendliness. Everybody would pass the time of day with anybody else. Even the boy crooks.

At noon on Good Fridays Gill would organise a special act of witness involving other churches and collecting musicians from St Mark's. The hairdresser supplied the electric connection and the Methodists lent their large wooden cross.

We formed a large circle in front of the shops and Gill would deliver the introduction in her lovely clear, warm voice. Passers-by were attracted. One Good Friday a youth gang leader cycled up provocatively to Gill, the very boy guilty of smashing her car window some time before to steal her bag. The thick wheels of the bike stopped inches in front of Gill at the presentation. With the presence of mind that only Gill could command, she stopped her introduction with,
"Hello Luke! How are you today? Bring your bike round here. There's room for you!"

Meekly all Luke could do was follow his minister's direction. But the words meant that this was a rare occasion for Luke to glow with a sense of belonging.

Gill, St Philip's, Tremorfa

Trouble with the Police

Previously Gill had arranged an afternoon tea for the local people knowing that single mothers and children would turn up to the community hall. Some singers from a local theatre group had been persuaded to provide entertainment. The occasion was not, however, very peaceful. Some mothers were collecting food in bags to take home. The rowdiness spoilt the singing and the singers left to change their clothes back in the church. People were uninterested.

I noticed the children disappearing, so decided to check. They were besieging the singers at the church and a singer's brother was trying vainly to keep them away. "He hit me," shouted a young teenager, "What did you do to him?" I demanded. No answer. And this is where bedlam broke out. The mother of the boy stormed and cursed up the middle of the road. An old car turned up with two uncles, who looked like Mafia men, leapt out and began to beat the

79

brother. There followed a police car who asked to interview me in the car. Thinking I was the culprit, the mothers gathered on the pavement waiting for me to be handcuffed away.

"Now can you tell us exactly what happened?" asked the sergeant.

I explained that I hadn't seen anyone being hit and, since I used to be a teacher I knew how to control my temper.

"Let him out, sergeant," announced the lady constable.

Disappointment from the mothers!

Later in the same day, someone had forgotten a coat so we returned to the hall to be met by CID who asked if we had a black sack to protect the shotgun they had found! It seems that our affray had been a minor occurrence. Gang warfare had taken place over the weekend!

Nicola's Problems

The church in a disadvantaged area of the city is clearing up to close for the day. It has been a gathering for mothers and children where mothers are seeking a coffee and cake escape and children are free to do craft work or even run wild. What are they running from?

A mother called Nicola appeared at the door.
"Is Gill here?" she asked with desperation in her voice and eyes.
Nicola is pale faced and her hands are quivering, perhaps under an influence of drugs. She seeks to preside over a family of three girls and one boy. The eldest teenage girl has wandered from a safe and good pathway and the boy, the youngest child, is an important member of a boy gang who seek to find someone to torment. Their home has been semi-wrecked by its inhabitants, so that one day the Council will have to board it up and move the family away.

81

The boy, Kane, (not spelt Cain) stood before the serving hatch fingering a knife to check how sharp it was. The helper asks for the knife with the handle facing him. Kane complies, the helper noticing as they exchange human looks the boy's need for love and security. He sees that the helper cares.

Gill would have lifted Nicola's spirit in spite of everything. No-one else could help Nicola as much as Gill, who had left on another errand. Nicola felt lost at the end of her tether.

So strength of character and power to love are painfully obvious in that person's absence. Perhaps only someone like Gill was brave enough to serve a church in such an area. She certainly hadn't ever flinched.

Hobbies

"It's all right for you," remarked Gill to
me one day. "You've got hobbies!"
This was true. My main hobby was music
– listening (while ironing) singing in
choirs, violin playing (or viola). In fact
Gill would proudly introduce me as
"This is Stephen, my husband. He's a
musician."
This remark always boosted my confidence and gave me a very satisfying job
in church services.

But my retort to Gill about hobbies
helped Gill to acknowledge she had
hobbies.

For Gill shopping was not just a
necessity. It took two days. The first was
to study the market, the second to know
where to strike. Bargaining also gave Gill
an excitement. She came home with a
memento from Mauritius billed at 600
(Mauritian rupees) but which she got for
100 and at the rugby match, by walking
away pointedly, bought a Welsh flag at half

price. Then there was gardening and visiting garden centres (for all sorts of items).

Which brings us to travel. Travel is dealt with in more detail later but it was also a hobby for Gill. She was a keen traveller but her trips weren't all holidays. She had been to Australia to lecture and South India to visit a Christian community. She had organised pilgrimages to the Holy Land including one very memorable one for St Mark's Church with others joining in.

During the relatively short time that we were together an impressive number of visits were undertaken. On our return from the other side of the world, where we were able to visit friends who were living there, Bob Capper remarked as we arrived back at church,
"Behold! These travellers return."
I lost count of how many times we had sunshine visits to the Canary Isles.

New Zealand takes twenty-three hours in aeroplanes but a nice stop was made in

Singapore where Gill, of course, had friends. What a memorable place Singapore is!

Bruges (twice) was a favourite destination. The first visit was in separate rooms before we were married. Gill took work with her and kept in contact with her churches on mobile phone.

Much successful and absorbing travel was undertaken in Europe by Great Rail Journeys – Lille, Frankfurt, Budapest, Prague, all with their special character. Even now I feel I am still meeting friends on St Pancras with all the anticipation and excitement that Gill could generate.

A Mediterranean cruise was undertaken. The Coliseum and the Vatican form a striking contrast. The climax of that trip was walking in the steps of van Gogh at Arles in Southern France.

Our flying trip to Paris was a great delight.

The Baltic cruise stopping at
St Petersburg was another world far away
that stays alive in memory. Holidays!
Holidays! Holidays! But what a
wonderful, vivacious deeply lovable person
to be with, one who could win friends
worldwide. Gill could spill her vibrant
presence to colour any gathering and
especially a party.

Another hobby to which Gill's family
house still witnesses is mementos. Some
are neatly stored. However, was there any
room for them all? Some of the origins are
unknown. Perhaps start with the Welsh
traditional wooden spoons (half a dozen);
wooden animals from Africa, New
Zealand, Mauritius; artistic Nativity
figures (at least three sets); ducks of
various sizes, jaunty wood – rare because
they are no longer available; photographs
and photograph albums (about six thousand
on an iPad); if you are not careful you will
jangle a cowbell (or two); a collection of
wooden tortoises; a Russian Fabergé egg;
the Kopenhagen mermaid - all walls are
carefully and artistically adorned. I will
stop here because I shall never be

comprehensive but I mustn't forget the two ballerinas in the bedroom.

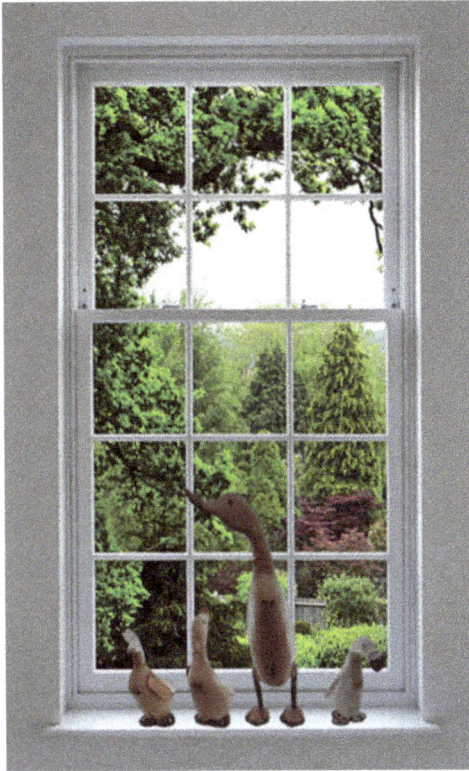

Wooden ducks adorn the windowsill

Welsh Assembly

Gill's work, even in semi-retirement, was made totally authentic and justified by her appointment by Archbishop Barry as chaplain to the Welsh Assembly. Since she was receiving a pension there could be no remuneration but the way Gill did the job was worth gold.

The sixty members of the assembly were visited individually and always supported by their chaplain. Gill's powerful faith shone from her presence and attitude – from her fiery, memorable personality and, by her own (later) declaration was 'practical faith'. Faith was never called religious because it flowed from her very psyche. When Jesus quoted Deuteronomy about loving the Lord God with all your heart, soul, mind and strength, was He perhaps thinking of the whole being? Anyway that was Gill's natural approach. She had a warm, wonderful, joyful and memorable presence. Of course, Gill espoused a rock-like theology but her sermons and prayers were all about God's

love for all people. As I write I can see her
fantastic, overwhelming smile.

*The Senedd building (right) next to the Pierhead
building, Cardiff Bay*

A Baptism

The family members with a baby to
baptise gather round the font, Gill presides,
her mellifluous tone commanding attention.
If you insist on immersion, please do not
stop reading. (A colleague of Gill's also
an Anglican with Presbyterian roots, the
Rev'd Rosemary Aldis, once declared that
the Anglican Church offered baptism by
sprinkling, pouring or immersion!)

In the respectful mêlée the service
progresses. One four-year old boy is
uncomfortable and lost. What's going to
happen to his new little sister? His parents
were a little embarrassed at his fidgeting.
But the padre officiant always has presence
of mind and takes the boy by the hand and
halting the ceremony briefly, she says,
remembering or somehow knowing his
name, "Come and stand with me, Robert.
You'll be fine!"

The boy becomes calm and belonging (a
very important thing in a church).

At the conclusion, a grandfather standing next to me turns and says through unchecked tears,
"This service has been a lovely blessing." What sort of baptism was this if it affected everyone? I knew it was Holy Spirit charisma powered via Gill.

David Bradshaw and Many Godchildren

David Bradshaw is an example of the
many firm, close friends that Gill made
throughout her life, men and women, boys
and girls. In fact it was always obvious
that Gill possessed the precious gift of
friendship.

At the same time, although Gill had no
children of her own, through becoming a
very young widow, and because of her
overwhelmingly full later career, she very
responsibly undertook many godchildren.
These did not live
nearby but were
spread in various
places where Gill had
been. Some were
relatives but all were
followed closely with
birthdays or visits.
The way Gill treated
these young ones,

David's son, Stephen's graduation

and, for that matter all children was, let's
say, rather like a 'mother superior'. She
always spent much time caring for these

godchildren and for all her many nephews and nieces. For instance, Gill always made sure they received Advent calendars.

David's wife, also called Gill, died young and Gill became David's prayer partner, a role which she kept up for the rest of her life.

David's son, Stephen, eventually a professional musician naturally became Gill's godson and she was able to hold the towel at Stephen's baptism. David was, and is, a Baptist Christian. Gill was also able to attend Stephen's graduation ceremony at Oxford and Stephen was able to play a very important role in Gill's time, more of which later.

Gill with godson Stephen

It might be worth noting here that Gill was aunt to five nieces, three nephews, nine great nieces and four great nephews. She sent Advent calendars every year to all her young nephews and nieces.

Happy Evening Service with Gill

For me, a previous life in choirs had meant that Evensong, especially the psalm, had been my favourite church service. With Gill the tradition of St Mark's made the evening service, yes different but differently absorbing and involving.

First the music was made with a small group – friends on violin, cello and piano, sometimes flute or guitar and with me on viola (or playing alto on violin). For the musicians this was a very enjoyable time, happily listening to one another and happily blending. Good friends took turns with readings and prayers.

St Mark's considered sermons important and quite often it would be Gill's turn. So preparation at home in the afternoon would see Gill on one side of the dining room table and me on the other, listening to Gill trying out her latest sermon. Occasionally I would forget that my task was listening and make some remark at the end about perhaps changing

something. The retort would be something like,
"I'm not changing anything!"

Listening probably represented possible congregation reaction or the preacher just wanted to see that it sounded like to her. In any case hubby was all admiration.

When the sermon came to be preached, I sat very proudly near the lectern listening to the real thing. It was always beautifully delivered, very engagingly presented, very well ordered and memorable. Professional, model sermons like Gill's were always good and every one timed to nineteen, twenty or twenty-one minutes, exactly as they had been timed in the afternoon over the dining room table.

Happy Days!

Perhaps, on the way home, we would call at Gill's friend Lynette's house to wind down after a long day. For vicars Sunday is always a long day.

Another Sermon

At least once a year *'Churches Together'* would meet for a combined service. One year in the large St Joseph's Catholic Church, Gill was to deliver the sermon which included important material about the church worldwide, the persecuted church and Gill's own experience.
However, Gill was recovering from a voice infection, so she told me,
"You'll have to read my sermon!"

I was meticulous, explaining clearly that it was my wife's, the Rev'd Gill Dallow's, sermon and I was just the reader.
Unfortunately this fact did not reach everybody. Afterwards people were saying to me,
"Thank you for your very fine sermon."
I kept insisting it was my wife's. Gill just said,
"I should have changed a couple of sentences in the middle!"

Retired Minister of Faith?

Some previous anecdotes have humorous innuendos with flashes of almost unkind irony. Do not mis-understand; the profound charismatic and truly Christ-like effect of Gill's personality and love for others is the main object of this story. It is here, first and foremost to honour her work and powerful influence of goodness and leadership that she showed in her life.

A summary of her amazing career can be listed thus. How she fitted everything in is a wonder.

1. Very successful teaching
2. Lecturing
3. Scripture Union Representative
4. Parish Priest
5. Carer
6. Wife (twice)
7. Running a church community - St Giles and St Philip's with curacy in West Ealing
8. Serving in St Mark's

9. Involved with three schools, in one of them as a highly valued governor (and friend)
10. Chaplain to the Welsh Assembly
11. Chaplain to the Sea Cadets
12. Keeping up friendships with widely dispersed people
13. Remembering in love every family member especially any who might be in trouble
14. Being a wonderful wife in later years
15. Membership of a leisure club to keep fit
16. Adventurous travel including a memorable trip she organised to the Holy Land
17. Member of the Nationwide Evangelical Alliance.

The list is endless.

Activities with Gill hummed – with everyone relaxed and confident. Gill had a special gift for choosing the right person for the job and also for making everyone feel they belonged, whoever they were, whatever age, whatever faith (or none) they espoused.

What motivated Gill the most? In
answer to the question "What matters most
to you?" which appeared on an important
medical form, Gill wrote,
"To live a life worthy of Christ and to share
faith in a practical way." *(Already quoted
earlier).*

This writer knows she succeeded.

A Difficult Journey

This journey began on Friday
6th February 2019. There are detailed
medical records elsewhere.

It is enough to record here how shocked
and overwhelmed we all were to accept a
diagnosis of a very serious illness for Gill.
At first there was the hope of successful
treatment by operation. We lived in this
hope for five and a half months with many
tests and appointments.

Hospital Lunch

The trolley with hot lunch and a kindly
attendant appears in the doorway of
Ward A7.

In the bed next to the door a woman,
full of personality with the middle name of
Margaret after her mother, has just had a
stent fitted to make eating so much better,
strides almost athletically from her bed and
approaches the man at the door with,
"What have you got for me today?"

This élan of joy delivered with such verve and even charisma affects the ward with smiles in the midst of sadness. The joy and inspiration of a moment is worth more than either past or future.

Note: This enormous hospital, The University of Wales (UHW) has good food and choice.

Dr Srivastava's doctoring care was exceptional. He knew more than anyone that we had to get on with the operation, which would take place with a team in Morriston Hospital, Swansea. Every Tuesday the team would meet to decide who was the next priority. With our incredibly supportive friend, retired senior nurse, Sue Morgan and Gill's incredibly supportive sister-in-law, we would wait in hope to be next. Why did Gill have to undergo so many appointments and tests?

Eventually the operation came which was eight hours long. Afterwards it was not good news. However, there was treatment and then palliative care. Dr Lloyd's attention was impressive, visiting or telephoning every Thursday. Gill's brother, William, and sister-in-law Lorraine, made sure we had a good Christmas in Gill's home. It was Gill's favourite time of the year. Gill's sisters Sue and Carol were devoted, as were her wonderful friends. Love really shows itself when the chips are down. Love grows deeply in sorrow and sadness. We all kept hoping and being unrealistic except Gill who said she had looked it all up on the internet.

Arriving for one session of treatment, a message came to say Gill was not well enough this time. It was during Covid so we weren't allowed into the hospital. One of the supremely kind nurses brought Gill to the entrance. There is no sorrow like the deep sadness in Gill's forlorn and beautiful eyes, a sadness which burnt my heart.

In mid-June 2021, our pharmacist was unable to supply an important repeat prescription so Gill's life-long friend,

Lynette, and Gill's brother-in-law Len set off to ask for help from other pharmacies.

I believe Len and Lynette did eventually find a pharmacy who could supply the prescription but before they returned, Gill died at 10.50am on 12th June 2021, with her family and husband present.

We needed to read something which was Habakkuk 3:17-end, the very passage that Bob Capper had read at our wedding. There is something holy in death and in this one it was overwhelmingly evident. Praise be to God for the faith, love and joy that Gill spread to all who ever knew her.

A Hymn of Faith

Though the fig tree does not blossom
  and no fruit is on the vines;
Though the produce of the olive fails,
  and the fields yield no food;
Though the flock is cut off from the fold,
  and there is no herd in the stalls,
Yet I will rejoice in the Lord;
I will exult in the God of my salvation,
God, the Lord, is my strength;
He makes my feet like the feet of a deer
  and makes me tread upon the heights.

Habakkuk 3:17-end

Thornhill, 29th June 2021

The slow, almost silent black car slid gently along the wide, imposing roadway. Very few words were being exchanged. The last place anyone wanted to be was where they were going and especially under these circumstances.

Elegant evergreens guide to the right spot all prepared.

A devoted group listen to the solo violin, Schindler's List theme which Gill had so often listened to from her sick bed. All are moved, and uplifted by Psalm 121. Because of pandemic restrictions reduced numbers stood in profound love and respect. Nothing could take away the deep human warmth that had been bequeathed to us all by one who was now 'precious in the sight of the Lord'.

I stood gazing down at the oakwood below and illogically wanted to adjust it. Charlotte, the undertaker, another good friend of Gill's, gently led me away.

When Gill was ill in bed, she would request,
"Play me Schindler's List," and I would oblige.

At the cemetery spacious and beautiful with its carefully chosen trees and position beneath Caerphilly Mountain, Stephen Bradshaw came with his father to play Schindler's List so that it filled the land.

When the oak was lowered I was unable to move. In answer to what my counsellor suggested I wrote down what I would like to have happened at that moment and this is expressed in the following poem.

Rainfall

We stood in the silence,
Lord, let it rain!
Forever that moment,
A never again,
Unyielding, final,
A now and eternal
With no word for our pain.
The music now silent,
Words only dull echo.
Deep earth gazes hollow.
Nothing to say; nothing to pray,
Dreaming of roses,
Petal by petal
To float gently down,
An all-time remembrance
With no wind and no sound.
Cover the earth, cover the ground!
Fine oak, bright gilded,
Sleep in readymade bed!
Scatter rose petals
Against grey sky sharp red –
Enough never the flowers
To honour the dead.
Tears in the silence,
Petals remain,
Rose petals floating,
Butterfly flutter,
Petal by petal,
Passion, compassion
Falling like rain.

Stephen Waters

108

Gill's Tribute, Lynette Veryard – life-long close friend

Close, life-long friendships are special. Gill and I had such a friendship. We prayed our way through the decades for our own lives and for our loved ones.

She was petite, trendy in her dress, a Laura Ashley fan, drove a smart car and had amazing energy. There were those who judged her before knowing her, so undervalued her. In reality, she was remarkably gifted, intelligent, compassionate and a peace-maker. For Gill, her calling to serve Christ in the Church was the highest privilege and greatest responsibility. Above all she loved her Lord.

Others she loved generously. Gill was brought up by a beloved Mum and Dad in a home where God was honoured. All her family were very precious to her – especially Carol and Glyn, Sue and Len, Will and Lorraine with their children. And Gill was much loved by them. There are so many memories that could be shared of Gill in family events; special times when she officiated – with joy at weddings, with kind understanding at funerals.

Gill knew grief when she was young; she should have expected a long marriage and her own children but lost Roger within a few months. He was a gracious and godly man.

In time, she wanted to marry again. Gill was perfectly open about this and engaged all her friends in the known Christian world to pray to that end. But, over the years, when a relationship appeared on the horizon, I would check whether it had potential. Gill would invariably say, "I haven't time now" … whether it was Barlestone parish, the General Synod or something else.

Then, ten years ago, the right man came at the right time - Stephen. Their marriage has been a continuing source of delight to me, as a friend. They were soul mates.

Stephen's daughters, Rowena and Ann, remember Gill – 'a radiant bride' – with love and gratitude. She reached out with warmth and kindness, ministered to them, and built caring relationships. Stephen's family became hers too.

Stephen and Gill shared mutual love, respect and companionship. There's a story of one of their early stays in St David's Hotel, their luxury escape, when so loud was their laughter late at night, that management requested a quieter joy. They enhanced each other's strengths. Few women have husbands who write love poetry to them and serenade with violin as they rest. (*Schindler's List* a favourite.) To complement the gifts I think Gill's strength of purpose took Stephen on 'adventures' he may otherwise not have had – and that included his support in St Philips.

Gill loved her 'flock' in Tremorfa. Her compassion and humanity – always evident especially with children – made the church the place where everyone was welcome and felt at home. She was always touched when a child - often on her happy visits to Baden Powell school – would call out, "Hello, Rev'd Dallow. See you on Sunday …"

She was an accepted part of the community which she served with the good news of Jesus' love.

Did you know that Gill Dallow is on Google? I didn't until recently. Her wedding photos are there and on the St Mark's website, her sermons. She was always a skilled communicator.

There were two words that Gill would not tolerate for herself: Retirement and Illness. Very sadly both became reality. She fought the gradual loss of independence and control; made worse by lockdowns. It was a heart-breaking battle. Gill did not doubt her salvation nor the certainty of eternal security but she had fully embraced the life God had given her and was reluctant to surrender it.

On family birthday cards she would write, 'The best is yet to come'.

Well, Gill is now enjoying the very best. Our times also are in the Lord's hands.

Please pray for those who remain grieving her loss – especially Stephen and her family and friends.

Gill is already greatly missed.

When I remember her, it will be fondly, maybe in tears but with a smile.

I commend her memory to you – pray that the blessing of who she was will continue to give glory to God.

A Tribute from Lindsay Brown

Gill was blessed with a formidably strong, determined and resilient character as well as an attractive and winsome personality born out of a firm desire to live her life in a way which was pleasing to God, which incidentally, many others also found very attractive. I first met her in the early 1980s when she was working for Scripture Union in Wales and I was working among university students. It was always great fun to spend time with her. She had such a vivacious character. She loved the Lord Jesus, Wales, young people … and, late in life, Stephen, who, she told me, brought her great happiness. I still remember her calling me on the phone when Stephen proposed to her. "Lindsay," she said, "I would like you to speak at my wedding. I think it may be a surprising challenge for my sweet fiancé when he marries me, so could you speak on the theme 'The blessings and challenges of marrying a Welsh woman'?" I duly obliged and at the reception spoke of three

114

benefits (there are more!) of marrying a Welsh woman. They were,

- Stephen, you will never have to worry about having something to talk about. When you come home after work just ask "What kind of day did you have, darling?" About four hours later you can ask a second question, "Can we go to bed now?"
- You will never have to defend yourself. Welsh women can be tigresses in defending their husbands!
- Thirdly, you will never have to worry about making major decisions from now on. Your wife will sort that out. Just focus on the minor decisions!

I heard many amens in the congregation including from the first Minister of Wales at the time! A year later I saw Stephen and Gill in a meeting. Stephen called me over and beaming said, "Do you remember what you said a year ago? It's all true."

A Tribute from Rev'd Bob Capper

I remember the first Sunday Gill came to St Mark's where I was vicar. She had come home to Baron's Court Road to care for her mother, so ending a long period spent in England in theological education, Scripture Union work and ordained ministry most recently in Leicester Diocese.

With a passion for the gospel, for ministry and for Bible teaching for all ages, Gill was willing to throw her energies into church life alongside being available to her mother. St Mark's around the time had a strong ministry team with vicar, curate, another retired minister, six Lay Readers and a children's worker, so ministry there was already well shared but some time before St Mark's had become involved with a parish in Tremorfa which was likely to close without some kind of intervention. St Mark's and St Philip's had agreed to enter into a mission partnership whereby St Mark's would try and find primarily lay people to try and bring some new mission

116

initiatives to the Tremorfa area. They were running a weekly Toddler group, holding monthly family outreach style services in the Community Hall linked to St Philip's, running children's holiday clubs and even a summer soccer school. We were also carrying on the regular Sunday morning Eucharist service though this had remained very small. Thanks to generous donations and part of the money from a sale some years previously of a former curate's house in Tremorfa, and the agreement of the St Philip's congregation, now fully behind the mission partnership, we were just completing a major internal conversion of the church building to flexible multi-purpose use. We had begun running a simple Messy Church event after school each Tuesday in term time for children who had to be accompanied by a parent with good numbers coming along.

Seeing it is a providential in God's purposes that the family home in Baron's Court Road was located not at all far from the Tremorfa area, the nature of the needs there, and Gill's experience in working as a vicar in not dissimilar areas, Gill was

117

willing to rise to the challenge of throwing her main energies into the work there. This was to continue for very many years and to be very fruitful. Gill built up contacts with families coming to Messy Church and encouraged them to come along on a Sunday morning as well, and soon the Sunday morning congregations were building up as well. Gill encouraged the congregation to accept services with a lighter touch in which families from all backgrounds could feel involved. She worked incredibly hard to make sure everything was ready and that people coming to church would feel welcomed. She would also invite the wardens to pray with her before the service, asking God to bring along just the right people to join the worship that day – often answered in clear, visible ways! We soon found that once the doors were open (and especially if food was on offer) there were people happy to come along to all sorts of things. She got a Bible study group coming, Church Council members would even bring their children or grand-children along to Council meetings sometimes and a real sense of community began to build up in the church. It was St Philip's church members themselves who had a vision to have a weekly Youth Club also on a Friday, and this was the first event not to be staffed by St Mark's members. Once more the church was transformed by the arrival of comfy sofas in the small room, and a whole raft of games equipment! With Gill's input there were baptisms, confirmation services, a Sunday music group with instruments for the children too. Gill enjoyed schools work and was a regular and appreciated visitor for Baden Powell School where she also became a Governor.

Fairly early in this period we discovered that Gill had a friend whom we hadn't met who was responsible for tackling the terribly prickly and overgrown hedge in the front of the church grounds! We were thrilled when Gill and Stephen married, and Stephen added his enthusiasm, commitment, musical gifts and a wonderful listening ear to Gill's own ministry.

All this time the weekly Messy Church activities run by St Mark's members (Gill

119

and Stephen always there) and also the
weekly Toddler's group run by others from
St Marks in the hall were continuing to
show our commitment to the Tremorfa
community and extend our outreach.

As well as St Philip's, Gill was asked
by the diocese in the early days to spend
some time at the Welsh Assembly, meeting
people and interacting and taking
opportunities to minister there and this
carried on for a little while.

Gill played a full part in the life of
St Mark's also, she and Stephen coming
along after St Philip's to take part in the
morning service, and then coming along to
the evening service too, taking part in the
preaching and worship leading and all the
life and activities of the church. There
were weekly staff meetings when we
would read the Bible passage for the
following Sunday's services and share,
plan and pray together. I particularly
remember and valued the fact that
whenever there were opportunities to pray
for the work we were doing, Gill and

Stephen would always be the first ones there.

It was good to leave St Mark's and St Philip's knowing that Gospel work was carrying on, and Gill's work in St Philip's, I know, must have been a great help as the parishes entered a period of clergy vacancy, and then the arrival of a new vicar. We were so sorry to learn of her last illness made all the harder by the restrictions of the Covid pandemic but rejoice to hear how bravely she fought it, so faithfully cared for by Stephen, until she came to her rest and return to the Lord. Well done, good and faithful servant!

Reflections on a Long Friendship (1976 – 2021) by Simon Holloway

I first met Gill Dallow at Redlands Parish Church on my return from West Africa where I had served as a VSO (Voluntary Service Overseas) in the Ministry of Education in Freetown, Sierra Leone. I had joined Redlands Parish Church soon after coming to a personal faith and first attended worship there in April 1971, a few months after my conversion. It was David Stuart-Smith, then IVF (now called UCCF) travelling secretary who had befriended me at the University Mission where I came to faith in Christ. He recommended Tony Baker and Redlands Parish Church, possibly because of their mutual connection with the Ewen camp ministry led by 'Bash'. Tony Baker had begun his ministry in Bristol at Redlands and as a part-time lecturer at Trinity College in 1969 after his curacy at St. Ebbe's Oxford. Tony and his wife Margaret became such good friends of Gill and she often stayed with them.

Redlands Church had a wonderful Sunday at Eight fellowship which met after the evening service on Sundays. It also took the name 'Koinonia', the Greek word for Fellowship and we did indeed experience much joyful fellowship in Christ especially for those in their 20s and 30s in these years in the 1970s. Gill was a part of this fellowship, which supported her while she served on the staff of Scripture Union as ISCF (Inter Schools Christian Fellowship) travelling secretary for Wales and South West England. She had worked as an RE teacher before this while living in Bristol at Colston's Girls School, now renamed as Montpelier High School in September 2021, after the statue to Colston, a prominent philanthropist but slave trader, was toppled in November 2020. She lived then in Wolsely Road in a top floor flat and she sometimes invited a group of us round for a meal or coffee.

During my own ordination training at Trinity College, Bristol, I got to know the people of Redlands Church well and Gill was part of that fellowship.

With a twinkle in her eye, Gill invited me and a number of other single men to support her in the New Year house party at St. Brendan's C of E School in Clevedon for 6th Formers in schools where there were Scripture Union groups. Not only at New Year, but also during the Easter Holidays, there was another youth house party at Legge House near to Swindon and we were also invited to support Gill with that event. During my first two years of training at Trinity College, I helped with several of these house parties and it was great to see Gill in action! She kept the young people engaged and mobilised us to assist with small group bible studies especially - all useful training for future ministry.

Gill then bought her own home in Wolseley Road, off the Gloucester Road in Bishopston and after I started courting my wife to be, Pauline, we often went to share and pray with Gill. She became a good prayer partner for us and we kept our friendship with Gill even after we moved to our first curacy in Wolverhampton.

After our first daughter Emma was born in September 1980, Gill was a natural choice as one of Emma's godparents, along with two other friends from Redlands days – Rosemary Boulton and John Woollam, who went on to train at Trinity College for the Baptist ministry.

On one lovely occasion in the nineties, Pauline and I were invited to lead a Mastersun activity holiday in Bodrum, Turkey. Our daughter Emma came also as our worship leader and Gill also joined our party and seemed to really enjoy the sun, sea and fellowship. It was a Christian holiday with short worship and ministry times every evening before supper, with a shorter prayer time, often with Mastersun staff in the morning before breakfast. I have a lovely photo of Gill joining the Conga dancing on that occasion. She also gave me some helpful feedback on an All Age talk which I had just delivered, to make it even better!

Both Tony Baker and I were present when Gill was ordained as a Deacon at St. Paul's Cathedral in London, but neither of us could make her priesting the following year.

We followed and visited Gill in every home that she moved to – London, Barlestone and then Cardiff – and one of our prayer topics always was a life partner for Gill! So, we were so delighted to first meet Stephen after Emma's Art Exhibition in Bath in 2009. Gill sheepishly asked if she could ask a new friend to join us for lunch on the Sunday and we were delighted to meet Stephen – an answer to our prayers over so many years. Gill also came to visit us wherever we went to serve in ministry and it was a delight to welcome Gill and Stephen to Cyprus and we joined them for a few days holiday in Pathos one year when they came to visit. We could not attend their wedding in October 2011, as we had just moved to Cyprus, but our two daughters Emma and Esther went in our place.

Gill was always passionate for the good news of Jesus to be shared with everyone and had a special heart for children and young people. She was good at encouraging and helping other people into ministry and taught by example. She had a great sense of humour, was fun to be with and believed in the vital importance of praying about everything. She had a wide circle of friends and was highly respected within Christian circles. She served on the General Synod of the Church of England, on the Church of England Evangelical Council (CEEC) and I remember meeting her at Blackpool for the last residential Anglican Evangelical Assembly in 2003. Sadly there has not been any such assembly since.

Gill and Stephen loved travel and made the most of their years together to explore different continents and cities.

They also served so effectively together at St. Philip's Tremorfa for many years building up the community of faith and helping to develop a weekly Messy Church and also eventually a youth club. She served as a Chaplain to the Welsh Assembly and gave so much time as almost a full-time vicar to the mission church of St. Philip's, while also being part of the staff team at St Mark's Gadalfa in Cardiff. She first returned to Cardiff to care for her ailing mum, but after her mum had her home call, Gill bought the family home, renovated and remodelled it and it has become a wonderful base even to this day for all Gill's travel memor-abilia, photos and books but also a lovely home for Stephen, his music and poetry and his occasional guests, including us.

We were so sad to say goodbye to Gill in June 2021 at St Mark's, during the Covid 19 lockdown. Only sixty people could attend her funeral, but we were delighted to be invited. A year later, we joined Stephen and family members at a Memorial Service at St Philip's, a very fitting place to celebrate her life and faith. May she continue to rest in peace and rise in glory.

Rev'd Simon & Pauline Holloway.
January 2025, Weston Super Mare.

This article appeared in
WalesOnline.co.uk on 7th August 2011

Vicar remarries more than 40 years after being widowed at just 23.

When Gill Dallow was widowed aged 23, just five months after getting married, she was devastated.

More than forty years on the Anglican priest is getting wed again after finding love at the age of 66.

Gill, now Reverend Gill Dallow, says love feels the same second time around.

"Someone asked me if it's real. Of course it's real. Love feels the same," she says. "It's the same process. You don't change as a person. It's no different."
Gill, Welsh Assembly chaplain, met widower Stephen Waters two years ago through the Church and they got engaged earlier this year.
"Excitement is in the air," Stephen says. "It's very exciting. You do get bowled over the second time around. I almost feel young again, it's rejuvenating.

This article appeared in the South Wales Echo on 8th August 2011

The Rev Gill Dallow with her future husband Stephen Waters who she met two years ago

Reverend finds love again after 40 years

Gill Dallow was devastated when she was widowed aged 23 – just five months after getting married.

But now, more than forty years later, the Anglican priest is getting married again after finding love at the age of 66.

Gill, who is the Welsh Assembly chaplain, met widower Stephen Waters two years ago through the church and they got engaged earlier this year.
"It's very exciting. You do get bowled over the second time around. I almost feel young again, it's rejuvenating," said Stephen who is in his seventies.

But Stephen was worried that Gill, who is associate minister at St Mark's Church, Cardiff, and works at the city's St Philip's Church, might be too busy to marry.

Gill and Stephen in Central Park, New York

And the former languages teacher admits his proposal wasn't romantic. "We were having a discussion and I just said, "We'd better get married then." "You'll have to ask me again," said Gill.

She and Stephen, who was widowed seven years ago, hope their story may offer comfort to others whose lives don't turn out as they expected.

When the then Gill James met first husband Roger Dallow in 1966 shortly after graduating from Bangor University, all she wanted was to become a wife and mother.

Tragically Roger, who she met at a Christian Union conference in Aberystwyth, was diagnosed with Non-Hodgkin's lymphoma a month before they were due to marry.

Although they'd been warned the outlook was poor they tied the knot at Metal Street Presbyterian Church in Cardiff in 1968.

By this time Roger was too ill to travel far so they swapped their honeymoon from Austria to Devon before settling in Hereford where Gill worked as a teacher. When Roger died the following February aged 28, she was heartbroken.

"For years you are in denial that you are a widow," said Gill, who grew up in Cardiff. "The first anniversary was a difficult time. The grief was dreadful. But my faith helped. Being a Christian you realise that's all you have, to hold on to at that time."

Gill threw herself into work becoming a high-profile member of the Church of England eventually being ordained at London's St Paul's Cathedral in 1996.

Two years ago she was working as a vicar in Leicestershire when her mother Peggy James fell ill so she moved back to Cardiff to care for her.

Gill took her mother to spend New Year 2008 at the Lindors Christian-run hotel in St Briavel's, Chepstow, where she met Stephen.

"Rather than written in the stars we believe God brought us together," Gill said.

■ *The couple will marry at St Mark's Church Cardiff on 14th October 2011.*

This appeared in *Woman's Weekly* as part of a *Real Life* article
(date unknown but around Summer 2013)

60s

'Married life is wonderful'

Reverend Gill Dallow is a Welsh Assembly chaplain. She lives in Cardiff with her husband, Stephen Waters, a retired teacher.

'The hope of finding love again never left me'

I married Roger at the age of twenty-three and within five months he had died from cancer. The grief was dreadful. My faith in God helped, but it took years to come to terms with it. Grief also gave me a far deeper understanding of loss and loneliness and made me determined to help others who went through such experiences.

In the years that followed, I worked with great zeal in education and was eventually ordained at London's St Paul's Cathedral in 1996, becoming one of the first female vicars in charge of a parish. I've led a full, challenging, wonderful life, but the hope of finding love again never left me.

Then, in 2009, my elderly mum became ill, so I moved back to Cardiff to care for her. We spent New Year together at a Christian-run hotel in Chepstow and that's where I met Stephen, an ex-teacher who had lost his wife five years before. We became friends – nothing romantic crossed my mind – but when my mum died a few months later, Stephen was a great support and gradually a relationship began to develop. We took a trip to New York together later that year and a lovely carriage ride in Central Park proved a turning point. I realised I was finding love again and that my new love was no different to the love I'd felt for Roger all those years ago. It was rejuvenating.

Stephen proposed last February. We believe God brought us together, so we married in the October at the Harvest weekend, which was the perfect time to give thanks.

Our wedding was a very special day. It was also a real church community event. The sun shone, the church heaved with more than three hundred people (including more than ten vicars!), tables in the church hall were laden with delicious food prepared so lovingly by the congregation and there was special entertainment for the children.

Stephen and I and the Reverend Bob Capper, who was officiating, put together a marriage service to reflect the fact we were in our sixties, but the love itself feels exactly the same as it did with both our previous partners.

As for married life, well, although it's been less than a year, it's as though we have always been married. We are determined to make the most of the years we have ahead.

The Baden Powell Primary School's Book of Condolence

Gill must have made such an impression on the pupils of the Baden Powell Primary School as the children each wrote a piece to put in a book which was given to me. Most of the entries were to thank Gill for coming into school to take assemblies and expressing their joy at taking part.

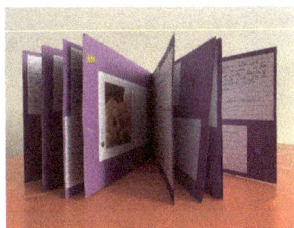

Here are some of the children's entries.

R.I.P Reverend Dallow

I remember when you used to come to our
School and teach us about god and heaven's...
We all enjoyed and appriciated you
coming to Baden Powell and telling us
all these amazing Stories.

Let your soul rest in peace ♥
You will be missed xx   Love Emilia

dear, mrs dallow

may you rest in peace and may the flowers
bloom around you whilst you sleep in your
fancy gold Coffin and thank you for
your fantastic religious Assembelys

your Sincersly, Cameron.

R.I.P Reverend Dallow

I remember when you used to come to our
School and teach us about god and heaven's...
We all enjoyed and appriciated you
coming to Baden Powell and telling us
all these amazing Stories.

Let your soul rest in peace ♥
You will be missed xx   Love Emilia

My favourite memory is when Reverend Dallow did our class assembly and when she used to read with us, and when she helped us make christingle oranges. I am sorry for your loss.

from Sofia year 5

Dear Reverend Dallow's husband,
I am sorry for your loss.
My favourite memory was when she made Christingle oranges with us and stuck things in the orange. Also when she brought books in for year 6.
It was lovely when she brought the advent candles in so we could count down to christmas.

From
Amelia
year 6.

Mrs Ceri Gibbon, Acting Head Teacher, also paid tribute to Gill in the book.

'It is with deep sadness that we share the news of the death of Reverend Gill Dallow. One of our hardworking school governors, Rev. Dallow

141

has been a valued supporter of our school for many years. We have fond memories of school assemblies and Easter parades as well as Christingle services in the local church, St Philip's, Tremorfa.

Rev. Dallow also helped to run Messy Church with her husband Stephen for the community, and was present at every leavers assembly to hand out transition books to Year 6 children. She will be sadly missed by all of us.

Her funeral will be on Tuesday where there will be a collection for youth work in Tremorfa and Wales in her name. We will put a collection box out in the playground and make a donation from the school community to say thank you for Gill's service to the school.

Should any children need support, staff will be on hand to offer help.

Rest in peace Reverend Dallow and thank you from Baden Powell Primary.'

A Record of Gill's Travel Destinations
(most of them)

Even the University College of Wales was a long train journey from Gill's base of Cardiff to which she eventually returned to look after her agéd mother – and also after many years of widowhood, to marry her second husband, Stephen.

Journeys were made to Australia and South India in connection with Gill's professional career and included, of course, holidays – the one before our marriage was to Thailand with a friend. Pilgrimages were organised especially to the Holy Land and elsewhere.

Many people read before going to sleep and may have a pile of novels under the bed. Gill had a pile of travel brochures. On return from some ambitious expedition, she would ask me where I would like to go next. Although I sometimes would be happy to stay home for a while, I would suggest somewhere I thought Gill might fancy; the invariable reply would be,

143

"Well, I've been there."

Returning from an especially long trip, Bob Capper, the couple's vicar announced, "Behold, these travellers return," which became the title of a photographic record, made by my sister, of the many voyages – travelling by boat, plane, train, bus and taxi.

The List

- **The Holy Land** (twice) – Pilgrimage
- **New Zealand**, visiting friends who had emigrated
- **Central Europe** by first class rail. The Harz Mountains, including a visit to Wittenberg on the occasion of the 500th anniversary of Martin Luther's Ninety-three Theses on the church door. It was momentous to stand by the pulpit where Luther had preached, visit the house and grounds where he lived with twenty-five students and a hard-working wife and to stand where he stood in Heidelberg University preaching reformation. You may also

visit the oak (it can't be the same one, can it?) where Luther burnt the excommunication letter. History comes to life.

- **Singapore**, visiting old friends in the Bible and missionary training college.
- **Dubrovnik, Croatia** Honeymoon
- **Île Maurice, Mauritius** Second honeymoon
- **New Jersey and New York** Visiting relatives with Gill's sister, Carol, in Granford. Gill and Stephen had visited New York twice before
- **Cyprus** twice) visiting Simon and Pauline, Gill's long term friends. Emma one of their daughters is one of Gill's many godchildren.
- **St Valery-sur-Somme** – a group visit. Some friends have a house in the area.
- **Sri Lanka (a garden of Eden) and the Maldives**. On one of the islands, the Imam was preaching over a loud speaker while the children went on playing, a group of ladies went on feeding the sea birds and shops continued selling to the visiting

tourists. A very colourful, rather worldly island.

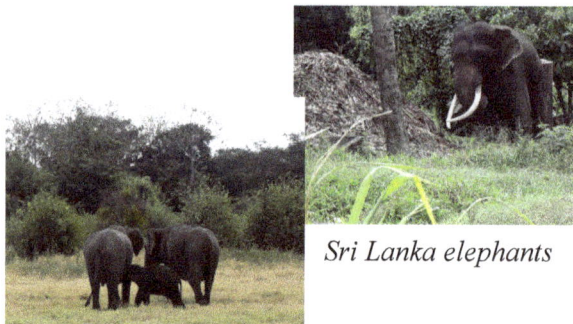

Sri Lanka elephants

Leicestershire should not be a long way away but it feels it by car on crowded motorways. It was here at Barlestone where Gill spent ten years ministering not only very effectively to her church and diocese but also to the community. We returned for Gill to meet old friends and for a wonderful party. The loyalty and love shown by Gill's people was a very moving experience for me.

Gill's reunion with her friends in Barlestone, with Stephen, September 2014

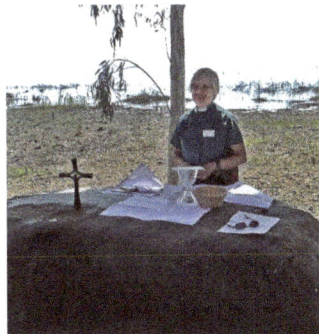

Not all our trips were holidays, of course. In February 2014 Gill led a group from St Mark's Church to Israel. She presided over an outdoor service on the beach.

And so in 2014 to Boston, America, an impressive centre for the best in American culture and civilization, (although the subway seemed complicated). It is quite fun to re-enact the Boston Tea Party and visit the splendid replica of the Mayflower. There is also a reproduction with historically dressed actors of an early pilgrim settlement. These tourist attractions are a bus ride from Boston at a place called Plimouth (spelt with an 'i').

In May 2015, we travelled to Central Europe by train which included Vienna, Budapest and Prague – highly recommended for those who love civilisation and history.

Tenerife, more than once, Lanzarote, (twice) which provided sunshine, Spanish and cooking on a hot volcano amongst many other delights. The architecture of Lanzarote, influenced by one architect, is very appealing. On the Northern fertile part of Lanzarote, a delicious white wine is produced and a flourishing Aloe Vera farm is run by an Australian family.

In spite of gloomy weather, a short trip to Paris was glamorous and memorable. There were two queues to see the Mona Lisa, la Giaconda - one queue for those with tickets to go in; the other was queueing for tickets. How long would be the wait? So with Dallow persuasion and initiative we were (with some debate) allowed into the exit door of the gift shop – the illustrious gift shop of that great museum, le Palais due Louvre where, of course, we bought a fine reproduction of the Mona Lisa, which now resides in the home lounge along with other matching old masters. Every trip had its memento. We stayed in a delightful boutique hotel, which also ran a clothes cleaning business downstairs. At the flick of a switch even the bedhead in our room lit up with tasteful, decorative lights.

Down the road was the well-known Madeleine Church where the ninety-six members of Llandaff Cathedral Choral Society had inspired a full house in the Madeleine with *'Zadok the Priest'* and other gems of music. Up the road dazzled the splendid – and very extensive Galeries Lafayette (and the Paris Opera!)

In the photographic record, the year 2016 looks more away than at home. Everything Gill did was ambitious and aimed at the best.

It started in the January sunshine of Tenerife. In March we were enjoying the fellowship and enchanting countryside of Lee Abbey next to the historic and beautiful Lynton and Lynmouth in Devon.

The Baltic cruise in June was so memorable and vivid. St Petersburg (once Leningrad) looked the same as when Dostoevsky wrote one of the best novels of all time: *Crime and Punishment*. I got lost in Tallin (I had also got lost in the vast station on a previous rail trip in Cologne). The boat was all luxury with only three hundred passengers and where

the staff numbered more than the passengers. Nothing is more peaceful than a luxury cabin where you may watch a summer sea wash gently and quietly past the window. Helsinki is lovely in summer. Stockholm is far too expensive.

Believe it or not, a week in the next month was spent in the totally wonderful Lake District, a visit by St Mark's Church to the Keswick Festival.

In October our fifth wedding anniversary was celebrated followed by (still in October 2016) a holiday in Barbados, an island divided into eleven parishes and which feels very anglicised. The following January we went back to Tenerife where we were beginning to feel at home, delicious walks along the coast or bus ride to the capital.

At the end of May and beginning of June 2017 we spent a short break in our caravan at Fontygary, Vale of Glamorgan.

One much prized photo taken around this time includes our dear vicar Bob Capper. How we do appreciate people so much more, when they have retired and moved away!

By July we were in the Harz Mountains in the steps of Martin Luther (mentioned earlier).

A bus trip to Windsor was memorable as long as the hotel room we stayed in can be forgotten.

St Lucia, a very beautiful island in countryside and sea shore seemed divided into those who worked for the tourists, who came across as well-dressed fluent English middle class and those who were much poorer with small, neat houses with a thriving chapel, people who frequented the lively local market.

We visited Lanzarote again in January 2018 with its captivating interest, contrasting landscape and very smart architecture.

We had visited Bruges before we were married but made a second visit, a town full of art galleries, picturesque canals, fine architecture, atmosphere, civilization. Goed Dag!

In May 2018 we returned to the wonderful Lee Abbey, with its beautiful countryside, exciting coastline, and lovely Lynton and Lynmouth.

Poland has history – Krakov, Oscar Schindler's Emailfabrik. We reached Auschwitz on 14th August 2018. Gill had always been passionately caring about the Jewish cause and deeply committed and moved by the evil injustice of the holocaust. The awful ARBEIT MACHT FREI at the gate had now become a tourist attraction. There was an ominous atmosphere created by the very nasty history of the place. As competent guides took groups around the horrors, their effect now in the past appeared somewhat alleviated.

However, suddenly a prison cell was before us, decorated profusely with roses. A large plaque surrounded by the roses told the story of Maximilian Kolbe in Polish and English.

Some people escaped from Auschwitz. They were caught and executed. As a reprisal the Nazi leaders chose ten people at random who were to be starved to death. The tenth man declared, "You can't take me. I have a wife and five children!" Maximilian Kolbe offered himself instead of the man and died in his place. Maximilian was a Franciscan Polish, Roman Catholic Priest who had already achieved much including learning Japanese and publishing Christian work in Japanese.

He was made a saint by the church and his saint's day was 14th August, the day we arrived at his memorial cell. Stephen was overcome and Gill was profoundly moved.

The man for whom Maximilian Kolbe substituted lived to ninety-five and visited the cell every year.

We visited Treblinka where there can be no memory of those who were murdered there except a field of large stones and boulders with the name of the place where the victims were believed to have come from. These stones cry out.

In 2018 we undertook a Mediterranean cruise which took in Rome and Barcelona. Most impressive however was Arles in Provence where Vincent van Gogh lived to complete most of his famous works. The café, asylum garden landscapes that he painted could be recognised in their reality.

Travel expeditions came to an abrupt halt early in 2019 when Gill became ill.

Nearly all of these travels were initiated by the vibrant subject of these reminiscences. Gill loved adventure, exploration and most of all meeting and understanding people and their back-ground. These travels were part of our

155

fulfilment of our marriage and of our joy in
life with one another.

Gill was a traveller of the world:
Europe, America, Asia including China,
Oceania, Australia and New Zealand.

A well arranged and presented
photographic record of these travels was
made by my sister Jean as a memorial gift
to me.

This obituary appeared in the Church Times on 6th August 2021

A correspondent writes:
The Rev'd Gillian Margaret Dallow began life in an area of Cardiff where streets are either given semi-fictitious Scots names, in honour of the Earl of Bute, or are named after metals. Gill attended Metal Street Presbyterian Church, guided by her father, who was a Moderator.

Showing much talent at school, Gill proceeded to Bangor, University of Wales, gaining a IIi in theology, followed by teacher training and a diploma in education.

Teaching at a challenging school in Pontypridd, Gill won her way to the hearts of those who had at first told her that they didn't believe in God and didn't want to learn Welsh; strapping youths wept when she left for a sixth-form college in Hereford. It was here that she met her future husband, Roger Dallow.

Very sadly, Roger died of lymphoma only six months later. Gill became a widow at the early age of twenty-four.

She moved to Bristol to teach at a girls' public school, studying for a higher degree at the same time, and becoming very active in Redlands church, mostly as an evangelist and mostly with youth.

Gill was a pioneer when working for the Scripture Union, setting up Christian Union clubs over a wide area in the south-west and in Wales and forming the Association of Christian Teachers.

Gill formed wonderful and lasting friendships. All recognised her vibrant, engaging personality, her strong deter-mination to see things done. One or two leaders saw her powerful spirit as a threat, but the wise knew to give her free rein for the good of everyone.

Having gained a higher degree, Gill became Director of Training at what was then the London Bible College (now London School of Theology). She wrote two books; *Touching the Future* was very influential and is still obtainable.

During her time at the college, Gill was accepted for ministry training and was ordained in 1996 in St Paul's Cathedral. She served her title, as a NSM, at St John and St James, West Ealing, where her vivacious nature and lively engagement made her stay very memorable. (Look up the *Sound of Dallow* on Google.)

Next, Gill took charge of the parish of Barlestone, in Leicestershire, and was also diocesan youth adviser. Gill's lovely personal touch blossomed in joys and sadness as she got to know most people in the community, befriending and bonding permanently with "those of the household of faith" and with others besides.

Obliged to return to Cardiff to look after her ageing mother, Gill went through a very stressful time with house moving, change of direction, and work.

The change brought an appointment by the Archbishop of Wales as Chaplain to the Welsh Assembly and also her recognition as associate minister at St Mark's and St Philip's, Cardiff. The first of these churches is looked upon as a beacon of Evangelical Anglicanism, and the second was that of a conventional district in a very disadvantaged area. Gill preached and served at St Mark's, but it was at St Philip's in Tremorfa that Gill had an outstanding impact, turning the area into a parish by getting to know everyone. Gill's 'network' of people and friends ranged from Members of the Welsh Assembly to poor children who had only wellingtons to wear.

Near the beginning of her return to Cardiff, Gill had taken her mother to a Christian Guild Hotel at St Briavels, where she met Stephen, a retired schoolmaster, who became her second husband. Gill and Stephen formed a special bond together and enjoyed great happiness.

Gill's lovely personality, her sunshine smile, her ability to form deep and lasting friendships, and her profound influence in so many areas are to be remembered. In all her trials, especially in the final illness, Gill's faith never failed. She remains ever, through her life and example, a fearless evangelist, a faithful servant of the Lord, and a lover of mankind.

The Rev'd Gill Dallow died on 12th June, 2021 aged 76.